Writing to Persuade

Grades 3-6

Published by Instructional Fair
an imprint of
Frank Schaffer Publications®

Instructional Fair

Editor: Cary Malaski

Frank Schaffer Publications®

Instructional Fair is an imprint of Frank Schaffer Publications.

Send all inquiries to:
Frank Schaffer Publications
3195 Wilson Drive NW
Grand Rapids, Michigan 49534

Writing to Persuade—grades 3-6

ISBN: 0-7424-1839-1

3 4 5 6 7 8 9 10 HIL 11 10 09 08 07

TABLE OF CONTENTS

Published by Instructional Fair. Copyright protected.

0-7424-1839-1 *Writing to Persuade*

Name_______________________ Date___________

SUBSTITUTING STRONG WORDS

Strong words and adjectives help create clear images (pictures) in the reader's mind.

Example: The three little kittens <u>said</u>, "We've lost our mittens."

The three little kittens <u>whimpered</u>, "We've lost our mittens."

Rewrite each sentence below substituting a stronger, more vivid word for each underlined word.

1. The teacher <u>talked</u> about eating healthy and its benefits.

____

2. The children <u>talked</u> on the playground.

____

3. This is a <u>good</u> candy bar.

____

4. This is a <u>good</u> composition.

____

5. He <u>ate</u> the candy bar as if it were his favorite.

____

6. He <u>ate</u> his food as if he wasn't very hungry.

____

7. The whistle <u>blew</u>.

____

8. The wind <u>blew</u> through the house.

____

Name ________________________ Date __________

MORE STRONG WORDS

Rewrite each sentence below by substituting a stronger, more vivid word for each underlined word.

weak words:
said
walk, run
eat

stronger words:
yelled, whispered
skip, gallop
inhale, munch

1. The children <u>said</u>, "We see a ghost."

____

2. The worried father <u>walked</u> around the room.

____

3. The children <u>walked</u> to school.

____

4. The stars <u>shone</u> in the sky.

____

5. The boy <u>cried</u>.

____

6. It is a <u>nice</u> day.

____

7. Time <u>moves</u> slowly.

____

8. It is a <u>hot</u> day.

____

  0-7424-1839-1 *Writing to Persuade*

Name_______________________ Date__________

WRITING SIMILES

A writer can combine two unrelated things to create a vivid image. When an author does this using "like" or "as," the new sentence is called a *simile* (sĭm´ ə lē).

Examples: She was frail, **like an antique clock.**

He is as hungry **as a bear.**

Create a vivid, descriptive sentence by adding a simile to each sentence.

1. The comet was like a bright _________________________________ shooting through the sky.

2. The lemon drop was as sour as _________________________________.

3. The volcano sat above the town like _________________________________.

4. Priscilla burst into the room like _________________________________.

5. The whistle shrilled through the town like _________________________________.

6. The box was as heavy as _________________________________.

7. The math problem is as complicated as _________________________________.

8. Manny drove the car like _________________________________ through the city streets.

   0-7424-1839-1 *Writing to Persuade*

Name _______________________ Date ___________

WRITING METAPHORS

A *metaphor* is like a simile, except it doesn't use "like" or "as." Metaphors create images by comparing two different objects. Look at the examples below.

Examples: He was **a hungry bear.**

   Her pillow was **a soft, fluffy cloud.**

 Create a vivid sentence by adding a metaphor to each sentence or sentence fragment below.

1. The hurricane was a ________________________________, which destroyed the town.

2. The streetlight was a ________________________________ in the dark night.

3. The fire, a ________________________________, roared through the town.

4. The snake, a ________________________________, lay motionless in the grass.

5. One lone flag, ________________________________, remained on the battlefield.

6. Santa Claus's beard ________________________________

________________________________.

7. The witch's broomstick ________________________________

________________________________.

8. His hearty laugh ________________________________.

     0-7424-1839-1 *Writing to Persuade*

CREATING SENTENCE IMAGES

A vivid image will often convince people to feel and act in a certain way. Pictures and descriptive words are part of this vivid image. Follow the steps below to create a vivid sentence image that supports the writer's purpose.

Writer's Purpose: To find a home for a puppy and a kitten.

Step 1: Think of words that describe the animals. Then use these words to write descriptive phrases. The first phrase has been done for you.

the home   <u>caring, loving home</u> _______________________________

the puppy   ____

the kitten   ____

Step 2: Use the phrases above to write one or two sentences that create a persuasive sentence image.

____

____

____

Writer's Purpose: To make the reader hungry enough to go out and buy a chocolate cake.

Step 1: Think of descriptive phrases and write them below.

the chocolate cake ____

the icing ____

Step 2: Use the phrases above to write one or two persuasive sentences.

____

____

____

0-7424-1839-1 *Writing to Persuade*

Name _________________________ Date _________

MORE SENTENCE IMAGES

Create two or three vivid sentence images to persuade people to do the things below. Remember to use descriptive words.

1. Buy a new sports car: (Picture a man and woman looking at a red sports car)

____

____

____

2. Take a trip in a hot air balloon: (Picture a passenger balloon lifting into the sky)

____

____

____

3. Eat healthy food: (Picture a young girl eating a delicious, healthy meal)

____

____

____

4. Go on a hiking vacation: (Picture a hiker crossing a long, swinging rope bridge)

____

____

____

5. Buy a life-size doll: (Picture a little girl feeding a large baby doll)

____

____

____

0-7424-1839-1 *Writing to Persuade*

Name_________________________ Date____________

WRITING SENTENCES TO PERSUADE

Vivid, emotional images often strike a chord in most people. These images on TV, in movies, or in newspapers can make us feel excited, scared, upset, sad, or sympathetic. Words can have the same effect.

For both situations below, use words to persuade people into feeling or doing something. Write three or four sentences for each situation.

Situation 1: You find a puppy hiding under a newspaper in an alley. The puppy is very thin and is trembling. Try to persuade your parents to let you keep the puppy.

____

____

____

____

____

____

____

Situation 2: You are a car salesman who is talking with a very stylish young male customer. Try to sell him a new car.

____

____

____

____

____

____

____

Name_________________________ Date________

WRITING A DESCRIPTIVE POEM

It is time for the annual Amazing Animal contest. The winning animal is chosen from poems written about people's favorite animal.

Before writing your four-to-eight-line poem, think of all the words that describe your favorite animal. Write these words on the lines below. A dictionary or thesaurus might help you.

_______________________________ _______________________________
_______________________________ _______________________________
_______________________________ _______________________________
_______________________________ _______________________________
_______________________________ _______________________________
_______________________________ _______________________________
_______________________________ _______________________________

Illustrate your favorite animal in the box below.

On a separate sheet of paper, write your poem for the Amazing Animal contest. Use the descriptive words from above to create a vivid image of the animal you chose.

   0-7424-1839-1 *Writing to Persuade*

Name_____________________ Date___________

WRITING A PERSUASIVE POEM

You have decided to enter the "Take a Family Vacation on Us" Contest. To enter you must submit an eight-line poem which explains why your family should win this vacation. The winning poem must express good reasons for needing the vacation. Each reason should be supported by a vivid sentence image.

Use the idea web below to organize your thoughts. You may add more boxes if needed.

Take a Vacation on Us Contest

Reasons My Family Deserves to Win

Adjectives That Describe My Family

On a separate sheet of paper, write your poem for the contest using your ideas from above.

Name _________________________ Date _________

IDENTIFYING APPEAL

Advertisers select their words carefully according to how they want us to feel. If they want to appeal to our emotions, they choose strong, feeling words. If they want to appeal to our minds, they will use smart, logical words.

Examples: The phrase <u>delicious cherry taste</u> appeals to your emotions because it sounds good. The phrase <u>doctor recommended</u> appeals to your mind because it sounds like a smart product to choose.

Read each phrase below and decide whether it appeals to your emotions or your mind. Write *emotions* or *mind* on the line.

_____________emotions_____________ 1. old-fashioned pleasure

_________________________________ 2. extraordinary, lemony flavor

_________________________________ 3. made from real fruit

_________________________________ 4. 50 percent more nutritional value

_________________________________ 5. more dentists recommend

_________________________________ 6. a sleek, shiny surface

_________________________________ 7. tested by scientists

_________________________________ 8. will refund your money

_________________________________ 9. discriminating people use it

_________________________________ 10. no artificial ingredients

FINDING PERSUASIVE WORDS IN ADS

Read the two ads below to determine their appeal—emotions or mind. Both ads are for Wavy Waffles, but they are written for different audiences. Underline the persuasive words in both ads that stress the appeal. On the line below the ad, write what the ad appeals to and why.

Wavy Waffles

Wacky, wild Wavy Waffles will bring a smile to your face at the breakfast table. The wavy shapes are fun to eat, and they taste great, too. Drizzle syrup or fruit into the waves and watch it slowly cover your waffle, one wave at a time. Wavy Waffles make breakfast an event. Plain, or covered with butter, syrup, or fruit, Wavy Waffles are sure to be a hit with the whole family.

Ad #1: It appeals____

____.

Wavy Waffles

The whole wheat and oats that Wavy Waffles are made of make them a hit with kids and a smart choice for adults. Made of all natural ingredients, they contain little fat and help lower cholesterol. As a part of your diet, Wavy Waffles can help you live a healthier, longer life that has a lot of taste. Try Wavy Waffles and taste what you've been missing. If you're not satisfied, simply return the UPC code to the address on the box and we'll completely refund your money.

Ad #2: It appeals____

____.

Name_________________________ Date___________

WRITING A PERSUASIVE AD

You are going to write an ad for Groovy Gum. Do you want to write an ad that appeals to the emotions or to the mind?____

List the words that stress that appeal. If you are writing to appeal to people's emotions, use exciting, emotional words. If you want to appeal to people's minds, use smart, factual words.

_______________________________   _______________________________
_______________________________   _______________________________
_______________________________   _______________________________
_______________________________   _______________________________
_______________________________   _______________________________

In the space below, write your ad for Groovy Gum. Use the persuasive words from the list above when writing your ad.

Groovy Gum

____
____
____
____
____
____
____
____

   0-7424-1839-1 *Writing to Persuade*

Name_______________________ Date___________

CREATING A TOY AD

Create an ad for your favorite toy. Use the word web below to organize your ideas.

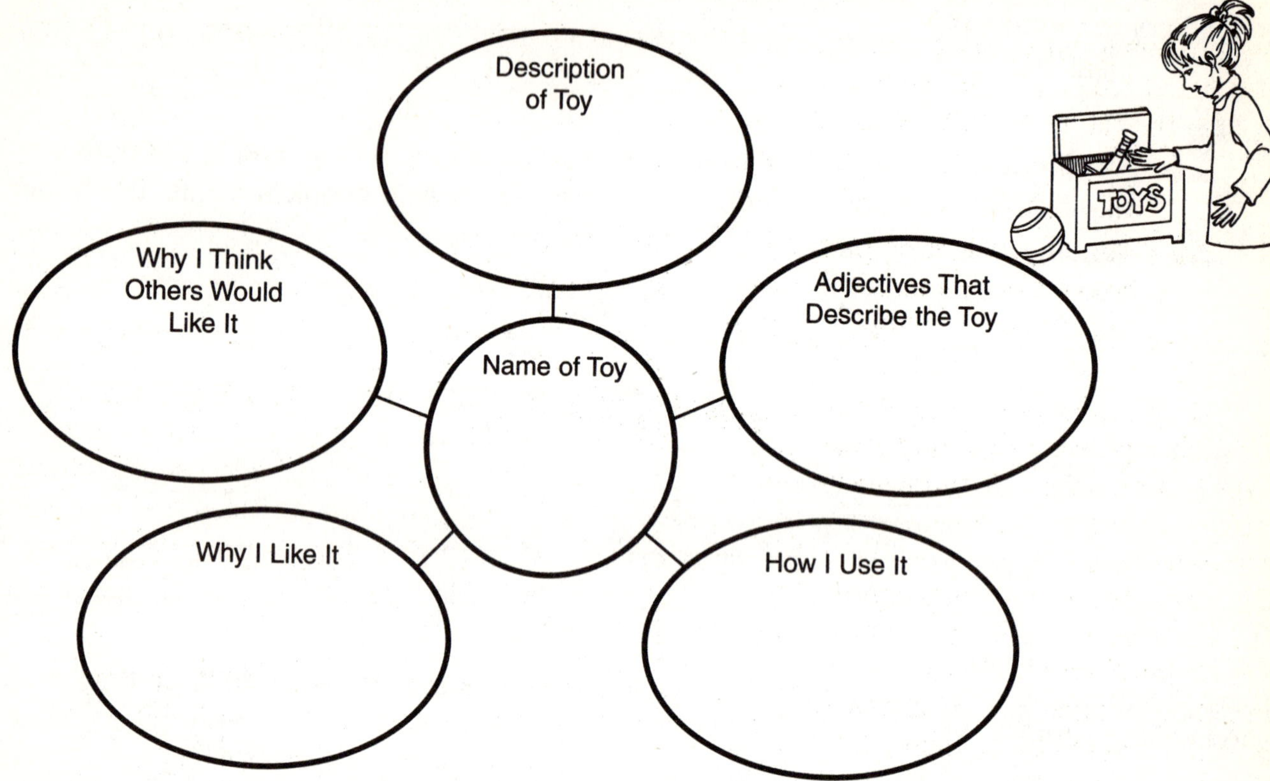

Will your advertisement appeal to emotions or to the mind?_______________

Circle any words from the web above that stress the appeal you chose.

Who will your audience be?

____ parent

If so, why should he or she buy the toy for a child?

____

____ child

If so, what age?

____

On a separate piece of paper, write the ad for your toy.
Include an illustration of the toy.

Name _________________________ Date __________

WRITING AN ANNOUNCEMENT

As a member of your student council, you've been asked to write an announcement for the new school spirit store that is opening in a week. Use the spider web below to organize your ideas and facts.

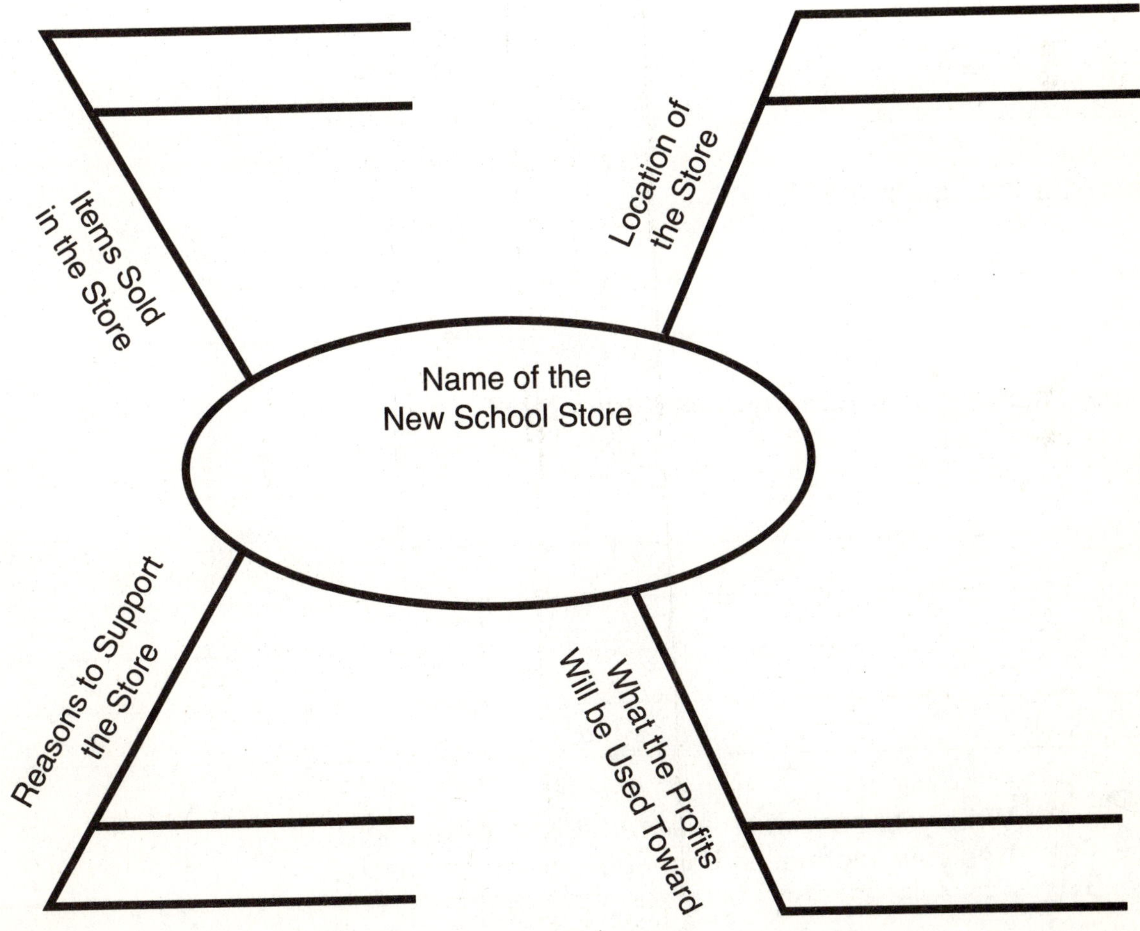

Use your notes from the web to write the announcement that will be heard on the P.A. system in your school. Use a separate sheet of paper.

0-7424-1839-1 *Writing to Persuade*

Name_____________________ Date_____________

WRITING A SPEECH

You are a recruiter from the Navy. You want to write a speech that will persuade students to consider signing up. Before writing, organize your thoughts below.

Introduce yourself—tell your rank and why you like being in the Navy.

____

____

____

____

What adventures will students find?

____

____

Where might they go in the Navy?

____

____

How would serving their country make them feel?

____

____

____

____

Write your speech on a separate sheet of paper.
Use your information from above to be persuasive.

Name_________________________ Date___________

CREATING A SANDWICH

The local submarine sandwich shop is having a contest to find the most wonderful, delicious sandwich ever created. The prize is $1,000 and a year of free sandwiches. Everyone is entering the contest, including you.

Use the organizer below to sort your thoughts and ideas before you make the prize-winning sandwich.

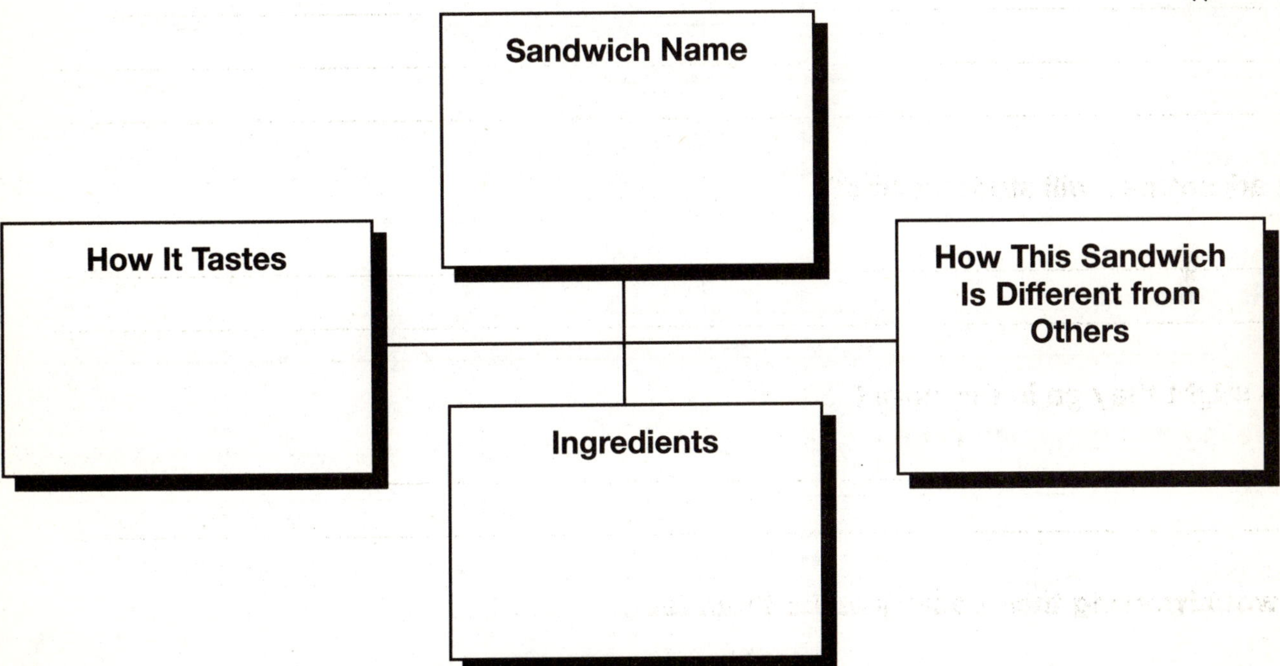

Describe how to make your sandwich. Use sequence words, such as *first*, *then*, *next*, and *finally*.

____

____

____

____

____

____

____

WRITING A RADIO COMMERCIAL

You have created your sandwich, and you want to promote it on the radio. When writing your radio commercial, remember that the audience can't see or smell the sandwich. You have to use strong, vivid adjectives that make your audience hungry for your sandwich.

 Write a vivid image for each of the following:

How it tastes: ____

____

How it smells: ____

____

What it looks like: ______________________________________

____

The feeling you get when eating it: ______________________

____

Illustrate your sandwich below.

On a separate sheet of paper, write your radio commercial. Use the information from both pages to write your ad.

Name_________________________ Date____________

ANALYZING DIFFERENT AUDIENCES

When writing commercials or advertisements, you should always consider the age of the audience who will see them. Each age group has different interests, needs, and concerns.

Your advertising firm has been asked to write three commercials for Smitty's Stringy Spinach. Before writing the commercials, analyze your audiences by completing the survey chart below.

	8–10 years old	15–18 years old	25–30 years old
Favorite heroes			
Favorite television programs			
Favorite hobbies or games			
Words to attract their attention			

Which two qualities of food does each age group consider most important?

- taste
- how it's cooked
- looks
- who else eats it
- nutrition
- price

0-7424-1839-1 *Writing to Persuade*

WRITING COMMERCIALS
FOR DIFFERENT AUDIENCES

Using the information from page 21, write three commercials for Smitty's Stringy Spinach. Keep in mind the age of the audience and what appeals to each group.

8–10 years old

____

____

____

15–18 years old

____

____

____

25–30 years old

____

____

____

22

Name _________________________ Date _____________

MORE ANALYZING AUDIENCES

You work for an investment firm and are discouraged by seeing people wasting their money. You want to create a poster to convince people young and old to start saving their money. Compare the two age groups below by answering the questions and filling in the Venn diagram with your answers.

What do they spend their money on?

Why should they save their money?

Whose opinion would appeal to them? (stars, investment bankers, peers)

What argument would appeal to them?

What pictures would appeal to them?

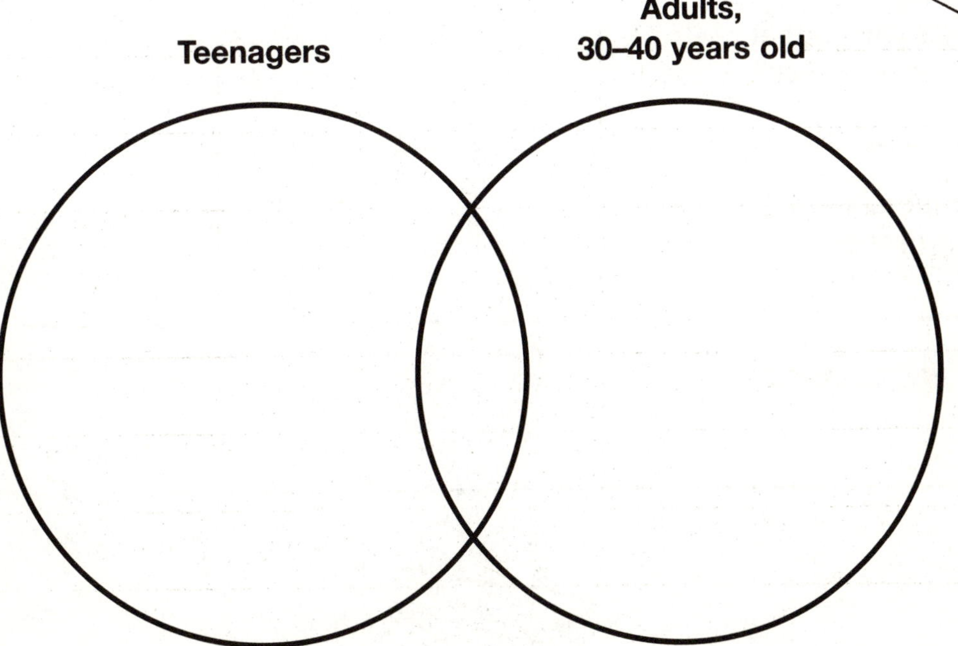

Design one poster for each age group. Use the information from the diagram to create an effective poster.

COMPARING AGE GROUPS

As a potato chip company employee, it is your job to design a poster that will feature a new potato chip. However, you have realized that you need to target young and older customers and this can't be done on just one poster. Analyze the age groups below by filling in the chart.

	8–15 Years Old	Senior Citizens
What do they look for when buying potato chips?		
Which appeal will work best— emotions or mind?		
What key words will appeal to each group on a poster?		
What types of pictures will appeal to each group?		
What slogans will get their attention?		

Name _______________________ Date _____________

DESIGNING POSTERS FOR DIFFERENT AUDIENCES

Use the areas below in which to illustrate your potato chip posters. Remember to think like your audience and design the posters with them in mind. Use both vivid pictures and words. Make their mouths water.

8–15 Years Old

Senior Citizens

0-7424-1839-1 *Writing to Persuade*

Name________________________ Date__________

IDENTIFYING REASONS

When writing persuasive paragraphs, it is important to use reasons to support your opinions. Using reasons in your writing is an effective tool and can persuade your audience to agree with you.

In the following sentences, underline the supporting reason. The first one has been done for you.

1. People should visit my state. <u>It has many historic buildings</u>.

2. Many serious accidents occur to small children alone at home. Small children should not be left alone in the home.

3. You must read *Women of the Wild West*. This new book by Debbie Dillinger carefully traces the role of women during the colorful frontier days.

4. Aunt Jenny's muffins are crisp on top and soft and tasty inside. She makes the best jam muffins in America.

5. Many teenagers have poor handwriting. Not enough time is spent on handwriting lessons in elementary schools.

6. Most children in our school do not eat cooked vegetables. Therefore, the school cafeteria serves only raw carrots and celery sticks.

7. Teddy is soft and cuddly. He is the perfect pal for any child. Every toddler needs a Tender Teddy of his or her own.

8. The Midville County Fair promises a fun-filled time for everyone. There are amusement rides, farm exhibits, and food-tasting contests.

Name ___________________________ Date ___________

WRITING WITH REASONS

Write a supporting reason for each sentence below. Use personal experiences, if possible.

1. Sisters and brothers always argue with each other.

____

____

2. Everyone should like spinach better than hamburgers.

____

____

3. Florida has nicer weather than Maine.

____

____

4. Dogs make better pets than cats.

____

____

5. Skiing takes more skill than swimming.

____

____

6. Watching too much television causes low grades in school.

____

____

   0-7424-1839-1 *Writing to Persuade*

Name_________________________ Date_________________________

SUPPORTING YOUR OPINIONS WITH REASONS

Persuasive arguments that are effective are supported by reasons. The reasons should offer solid evidence to support your position.

Support each opinion below with three strong reasons. Write in complete sentences.

Bike riders should wear helmets.

Reasons:

a. ____

b. ____

c. ____

The school year should be longer.

Reasons:

a. ____

b. ____

c. ____

____ is the best show on TV.

(Fill in your favorite show)

Reasons:

a. ____

b. ____

c. ____

_________________________________ is the hardest subject in school for me.

(Fill in a subject of school)

Reasons:

a. ____

b. ____

c. ____

Name_______________________ Date___________

SUPPORTING YOUR OWN OPINION

On the following lines, write an opinion that you feel strongly about. Your opinion could be about changes you would like made at home or in school. Your opinion could be about something that is happening in your town or the world.

My Opinion

I think

____
____
____
____
____
____

Supporting Reason

____
____
____
____
____

Supporting Reason

____
____
____
____
____

Supporting Reason

____
____
____
____
____

On a separate sheet of paper, write a persuasive paragraph that convinces others to agree with your opinion. Use the information from above.

 0-7424-1839-1 *Writing to Persuade*

CONVINCING A FRIEND TO TRY NEW FOODS

Your friend, Howard, is very stubborn and doesn't like to try new things. He especially doesn't like to try new fruits or vegetables. He will eat only one vegetable and absolutely no fruit. You feel that this isn't a very healthy way for Howard to live. You are concerned for him. You have tried talking to him about it before, but he insists that he is healthy. You don't agree.

Write a paragraph to Howard persuading him to change his stubborn ways. Support your opinion with reasons.

Before you write your paragraph, organize your thoughts below using notes.

Opening sentence:

____

____

____

Reasons for Howard to change his eating habits:

1. ____

2. ____

3. ____

Closing statement (be persuasive):

____

____

____

____

On a separate sheet of paper, organize your notes into a paragraph.

Name _________________________ Date __________

CREATIVE REASONING

Your sixteenth birthday is only two months away, and you can't wait to drive on your own. The only problem is that anytime you will want to go somewhere, you will have to ask to borrow your parents' car. Some of your friends have their own cars and can come and go whenever they want. You haven't talked to your parents about wanting your own car, but you want to.

Before approaching them, think about your reasons for wanting a car. Organize your thoughts below. Use examples to support your reasons.

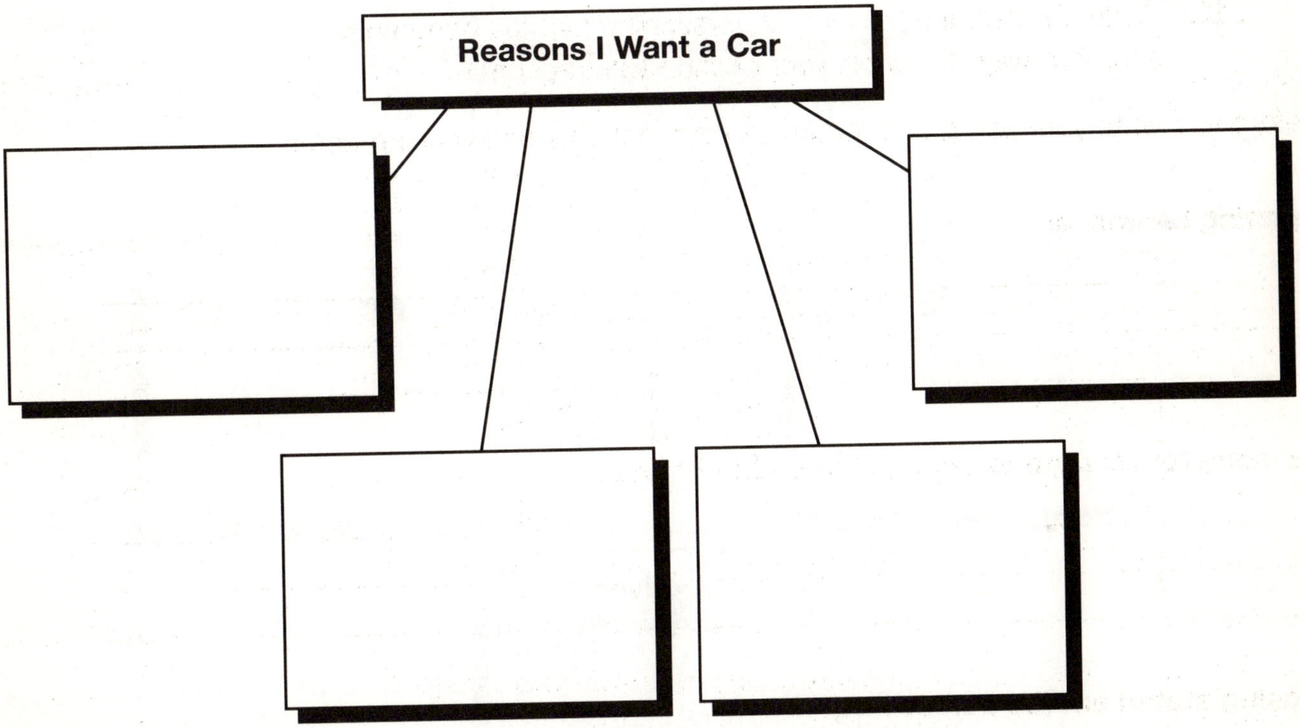

Reasons I Want a Car

Use the information above to write a persuasive paragraph that you will read to your parents.

    0-7424-1839-1 *Writing to Persuade*

Name_______________________ Date____________________

DESIGNING A FLIER

The school year has just ended, and you have a great idea for a summer job. You love dogs and want to start a dog-walking business. A good way to begin is by designing a flier to pass out to your neighbors that describes you and your services. Use the map below to organize your information before you design the flier.

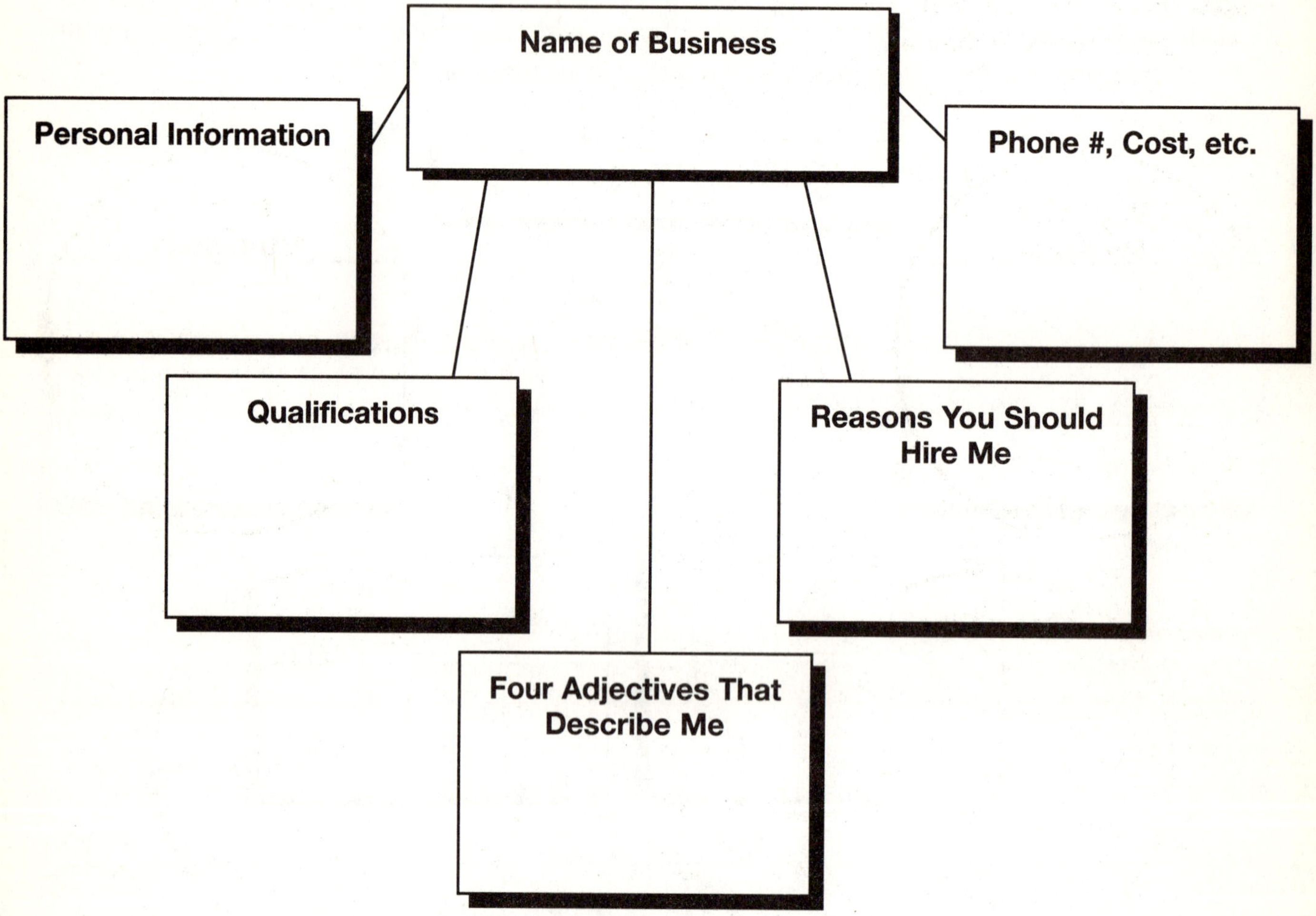

Name of Business

Personal Information

Phone #, Cost, etc.

Qualifications

Reasons You Should Hire Me

Four Adjectives That Describe Me

On a separate sheet of paper, design your flier using persuasive words and illustrations.

0-7424-1839-1 *Writing to Persuade*

Name _______________________ Date __________

PLANNING A TOURIST BROCHURE

Your class just finished studying the state you live in. Instead of giving you a multiple-choice test, your teacher has asked you to design a travel brochure for your state. She wants specific information in your brochure.

Fill in the state web below. Then use the brochure on page 34 to create your own brochure. You may add more circles if needed.

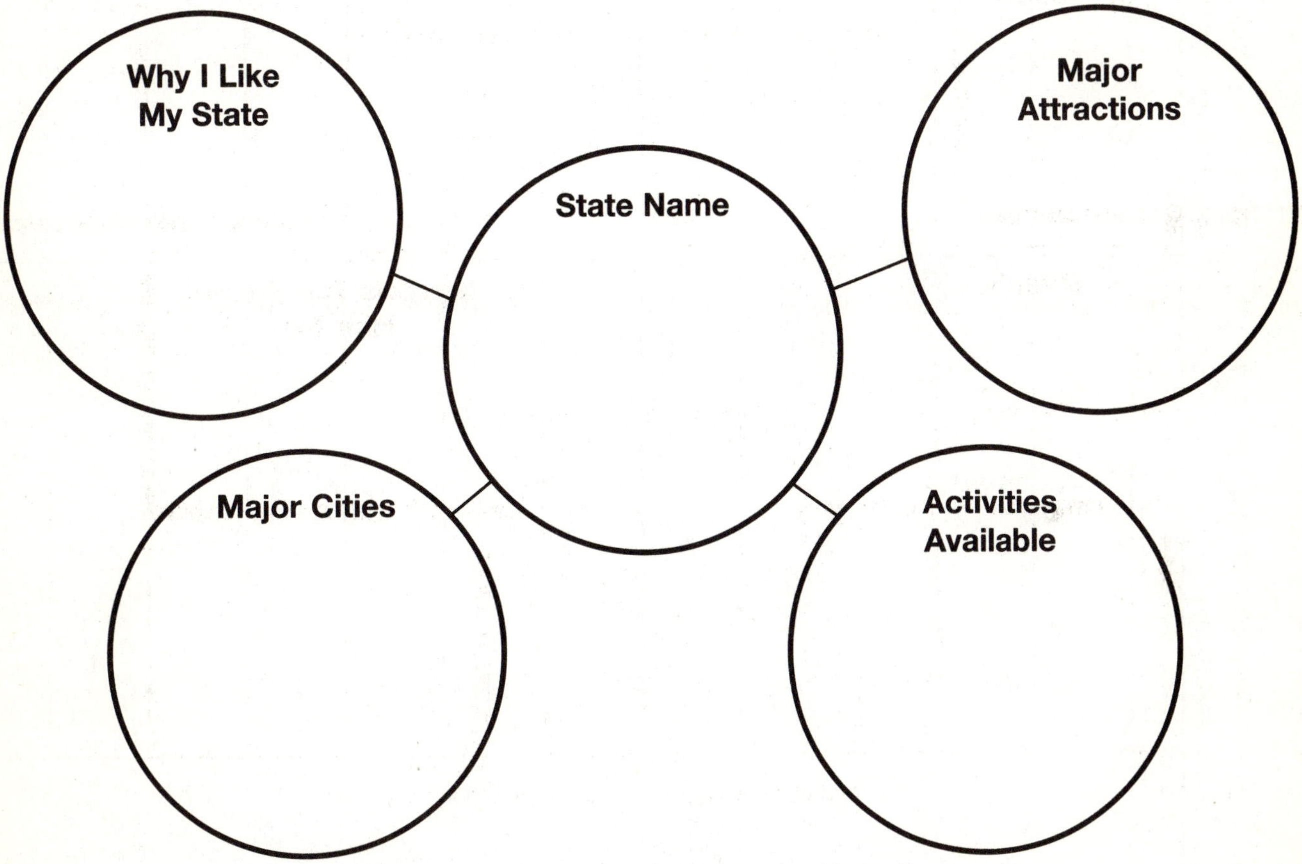

Why I Like My State

Major Attractions

State Name

Major Cities

Activities Available

Name _________________________ Date __________

DESIGNING A TOURIST BROCHURE

Using your notes from Planning a Tourist Brochure, design a brochure on this page. Be sure to give persuasive reasons for visiting your state. Write in complete sentences. Illustrate the cover. Then cut along the outside and fold.

Write about activities available and why people should visit the state.

Highlight the weather, cities and attractions.

Design the cover.

Fold

Fold

Name _______________________ Date _______________

ANALYZING HOLIDAYS

The governor of your state has decided that there are too many holidays. Because he cannot decide which one to eliminate, he is sponsoring a writing contest to allow school children to help him decide.

Before you choose a holiday to recommend, fill in the chart below with information about your two favorite and two least favorite holidays.

Holiday	Why We Celebrate It	Why It's Important to Me	What I Would Miss If It Was Eliminated
Favorite Holiday			
Favorite Holiday			
Least Favorite Holiday			
Least Favorite Holiday			

0-7424-1839-1 *Writing to Persuade*

ELIMINATING A HOLIDAY

Review your notes on holidays from page 35. Select the holiday that you want eliminated from the calendar. Write three reasons for your choice.

1. ____

2. ____

3. ____

Now write a persuasive paragraph supporting your choice. Use the business letter form below and address the letter to your governor.

Name________________________ Date__________

REQUESTING A CHAPERONE

Your science class is going on a field trip and needs a few chaperones. Your uncle loves science and used to teach high school science classes. You think he would love to come.

Write a friendly letter asking your uncle to be a chaperone on the field trip. Use persuasive words. Use the chart below to organize your information before you begin writing.

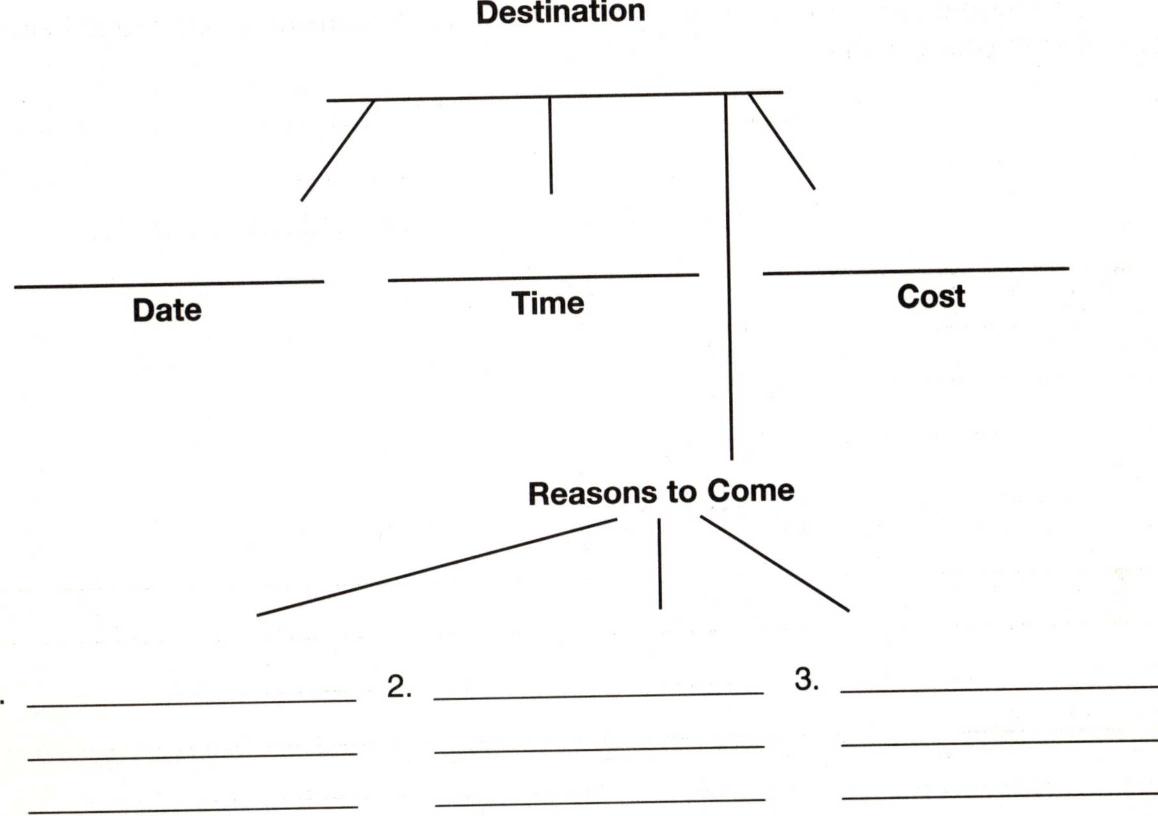

Now write the letter to your uncle using correct letter form.

   0-7424-1839-1 *Writing to Persuade*

REQUESTING A GUEST SPEAKER

Your school's annual career day is only a few weeks away. Your teacher has asked you to think of someone who has a job that your classmates would like learning about. Your assignment is to write a letter to this person persuading him or her to be a guest speaker. Before beginning your letter, make some notes below.

1. **To whom will you write?** _______________________________________

2. **His or her address is:** _______________________________________

3. **What is this person's job or occupation?** _______________________

____

4. **Why do you think this person would be a good guest speaker on career day?**

a. ____

b. ____

c. ____

5. **What information about his or her job would your classmates like hearing about?**

a. ____

b. ____

c. ____

On a separate sheet of paper, write your letter. Use the correct friendly letter form.

Name _______________________ Date _______________

WRITING A THANK-YOU LETTER

Your school's career day was a huge success. Your guest came and gave a wonderful presentation on his or her career. Your guest even offered to take your entire class on a tour of his or her offices. On the lines below, write a thank-you letter to your guest. In your letter give at least three reasons you think everyone was glad he or she came.

0-7424-1839-1 *Writing to Persuade*

DEFENDING YOUR FAVORITE TELEVISION SHOW

A network television station is planning to drop your favorite TV show. Because you think it is so good, you decide to write a letter to the people at the station persuading them to keep your favorite show on the air.

Before writing your letter, think through your argument carefully and fill in the chart below.

Name of the Show

____

Why It Is My Favorite Show

____

____

Three Reasons for Not Cancelling the Show

1. _____________ 2. _____________ 3. _____________

_____________ _____________ _____________

_____________ _____________ _____________

Adjectives That Describe the Show

_____________ _____________ _____________

On a separate piece of paper, write a business letter to the network asking that your favorite television show not be dropped. Use the arguments you developed above.

Name_________________________ Date_____________

DEVELOPING A TELEVISION SHOW

You saw an ad that was asking for people to submit ideas for a new TV show. The audience they want to reach is elementary students. You have a great idea and want to submit it. Organize your facts below before sending in your idea.

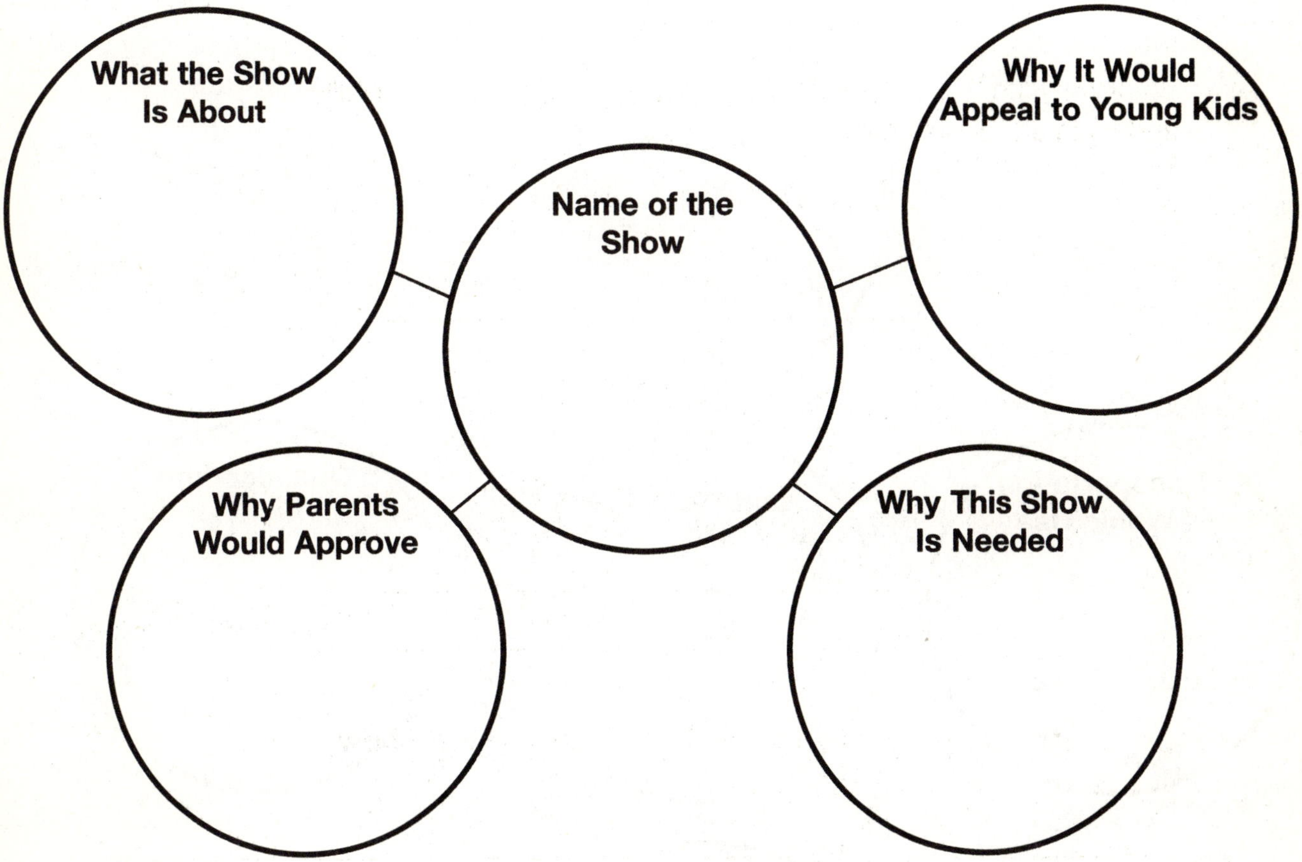

What the Show Is About

Name of the Show

Why It Would Appeal to Young Kids

Why Parents Would Approve

Why This Show Is Needed

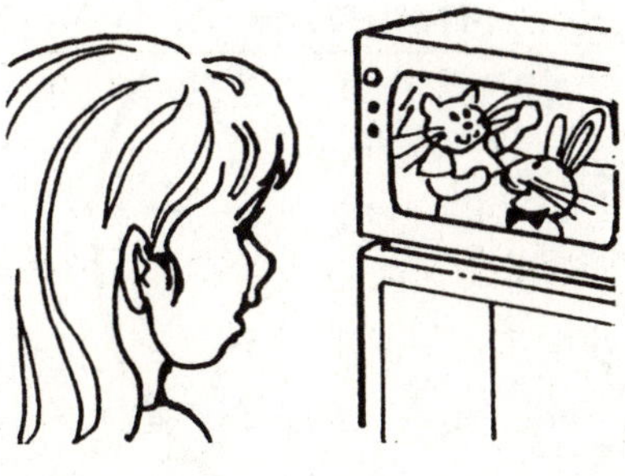

On a separate piece of paper, write your letter proposing the new television show. Use your information from above to write the letter. Be persuasive!

APPLYING FOR A JOB

You want to earn some spending money, and there is an opening for a newspaper delivery person in your town. You want to apply for the job. In the organizer below, record information that qualifies you for the job.

- Why I Want the Job
- Transportation I Would Use
- Name and Age
- Qualifications
- References
  1.
  2.

On a separate sheet of paper, write your letter to the newspaper. Be persuasive—you want them to hire you.

Name _______________________ Date _____________

WRITING TO THE
MAYOR OF YOUR CITY

In your town there is a beautiful park on a lake where you and your friends play. On the weekends, you and your dog walk there and play fetch. Boats sail on the lake in the summer, and families ice skate on it in the winter. A developer, though, sees this park as a great spot to build apartments.

You feel so strongly about keeping it a park that you want to write a letter to the mayor. Organize your thoughts below before writing the letter.

Write an opening sentence that asks the mayor not to sell the land.

____

____

List three reasons you want the park to remain as it is.

a. ____

b. ____

c. ____

Write two or three sentences about a favorite memory you have about the park. Be sure to create a vivid image for the mayor.

____

____

____

____

____

On a separate piece of paper, write a letter to your mayor persuading him to stop the developer.

Name_________________________ Date__________

WRITING TO AN AUTHOR

One of your favorite books doesn't end the way you wish it would.
You have created an ending that you think is much better. Write a letter
to the author explaining how you would like the book to end.

Start by explaining what you like about the book and write about your favorite parts. Then explain your new ending and why you think the book should end this way.

I Like This Book Because...

Favorite Parts

Title and Author

New Ending

I Think This Ending is Better Because...

Now you are ready to write your letter on a separate piece of paper. Your letter should include the information you have written above.

0-7424-1839-1 *Writing to Persuade*

Name ___________________________ Date _____________

A DIFFERENT KIND OF BOOK REPORT

You have just read a fantastic book and would like to share it with a friend. Fill in the blanks below about the book.

Title: ___________________________

____

Author: ___________________________

____

Setting: ___________________________

____

Problem or Conflict: ___________

____

**DON'T GIVE AWAY
THE ENDING!**

Characters I Like:

____

____

____

Reasons to Read the Book

1. ___________________________

2. ___________________________

3. ___________________________

On a separate sheet of paper, write a letter to your friend urging him or her to read the book.

   0-7424-1839-1 *Writing to Persuade*

DISAGREEING WITH A CHARACTER

Think of a book you have read in which a character made a decision you didn't agree with. Write a letter to this character explaining why you disagreed with his or her decision. Then tell the character what you would have done instead. Try to persuade the character to feel that your decision is a better one. Organize your thoughts below.

Title: ____

Author: ____

Character's name: ____

What was the character's decision? ________________________

____

____

____

List two reasons stating why you disagree with the character's decision.

1. ____

2. ____

What decision would you recommend instead? ________________

List two reasons stating why your decision would be a better one.

1. ____

2. ____

Name_______________________ Date____________

WRITING ABOUT A
CHARACTER'S PROBLEM

Use your notes on page 46 to write a letter to the character you have chosen. In the letter, try to persuade him or her to solve the problem by following your advice. In the first paragraph, explain why you are writing to this character. Then explain why you disagree with a decision the character made. In the second paragraph, persuade him or her to feel that your decision is a better one. Use reasons to support your opinion.

0-7424-1839-1 *Writing to Persuade*

Name _______________________ Date _______________

IDENTIFYING REASONS AND SUPPORTING EXAMPLES

When writing persuasive sentences, it is important to support your opinions with reasons. This helps grab the reader's attention and support your argument. To make your writing even more effective, use examples in your sentences that describe your reasons.

Look at the sentences below. Each sentence has an opinion, a persuading reason, and an example to support the reason. Draw one line under the persuading reason, and draw a box around the supporting example.

Example: **If you want to be a weight lifter, you should drink three glasses of milk each day. Milk is a major source of calcium, which is needed for strong bones. Alfonso Lewis, a world champion weight lifter, drinks three glasses of milk every day.**

1. People should not litter. It costs taxpayers thousands of dollars each week to clean up the litter. Our town spends $2,000 a week to keep our streets clean.

2. Japanese children go to school six days a week. American school children should also go to school six days a week. This would give students more time to master all the lessons they must learn.

3. Because our school population is growing, our school needs more lockers. This year, sixteen students have to share lockers.

4. Everybody should have a garden. Fresh-grown food tastes better. My family will eat beets only if they are picked fresh from the garden.

5. Everyone should collect stamps. It is quite a profitable hobby. A stamp my uncle bought ten years ago for twenty cents just sold for $30.00.

Name _____________________ Date _________

MORE REASONS AND SUPPORTING EXAMPLES

Use reasons to support your opinions when writing a persuasive paragraph and you will be more likely to persuade your audience. Include specific facts and examples in your writing and your paragraphs will be even more effective.

Read the following paragraph. Identify the author's opinion and write it on the lines below. The author supports her opinion with reasons and examples or facts. Find the reasons and examples and write them below.

Although many students complain about going to school, I think school is a good place to be. I enjoy learning new facts and ideas. Just last week my teacher explained to us that people now believe Christopher Columbus was not the first person to discover America. In some of the New England states and Canada, archeologists have found remnants of Viking ships and weapons. Historians now say that the Vikings probably explored the seacoast of America many years before Columbus did. School also can be a caring place. When I was out of school with a broken leg, my classmates made me a gigantic get-well card. When I returned to school, my teacher spent her lunch hour teaching me the new work I had missed. I especially like school because my friends are there. I get to play and talk with them every day during recess and lunch. I think my days would be boring without school.

Author's opinion: _______________________

____

Reason #1: _______________________________

Examples: _______________________________

____

Reason #2: _______________________________

Examples: _______________________________

____

Reason #3: _______________________________

Examples: _______________________________

____

WRITING WITH EXAMPLES

Think about your favorite season of the year. What makes this season your favorite? What are some things you enjoy doing during this time of year?

Use the map below to organize your thoughts about your favorite season. Start by identifying three reasons you chose this as your favorite season. Then support each reason with one example or fact.

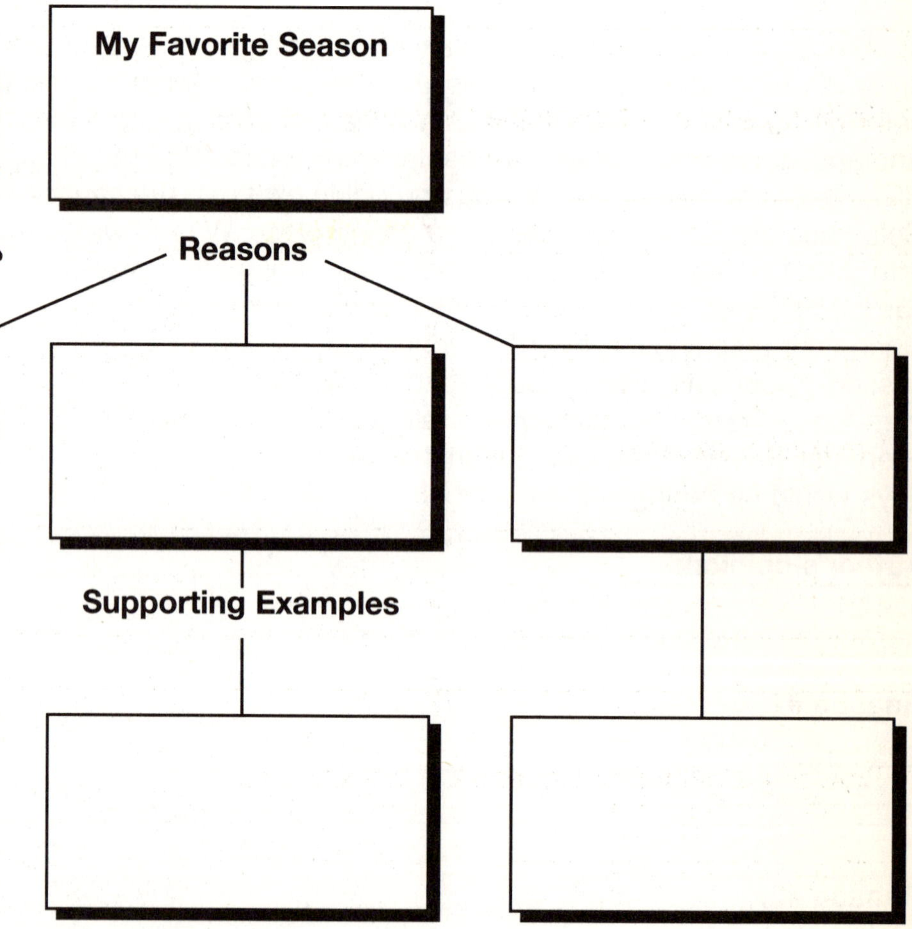

My Favorite Season

Reasons

Supporting Examples

Use your reasons and examples from above to write a paragraph on another sheet of paper. Explain why this season is your favorite. Persuade us to agree with you that this season is wonderful.

Name _________________________ Date _____________

WRITING WITH EXAMPLES AGAIN

Below are four reasons that students should not smoke. Think of examples or facts to support each reason. Write your examples or facts on the lines below each reason. Be sure to write in complete sentences.

1. Smoking is bad for your health.

____

____

____

____

2. Smoking sets a bad example for younger children.

____

____

____

____

3. Smoking is expensive.

____

____

____

____

4. Smoking is habit forming, and it is hard to quit.

____

____

____

____

 0-7424-1839-1 *Writing to Persuade*

PERSUADING STUDENTS NOT TO SMOKE

The Student Council in your school is sponsoring a "No Smoking" campaign. All the students in grades 4, 5, and 6 will be asked to sign a pledge that they will not start smoking. To kick off the campaign, there will be an essay contest. The topic is "Why Students Should Not Start Smoking." The winner will receive ten free passes to the local movie theater.

You want to enter the contest. Write a paragraph that has at least three good reasons to not start smoking. Be sure to support each reason with good examples or facts. You can use your reasons and details from page 51.

Why Students Should Not Start Smoking

____

____

____

____

____

____

____

____

____

____

____

____

____

Name _________________________ Date ___________

BANNING AN INVENTION

Read the persuasive paragraph below. Then answer the questions that follow.

The world is becoming too cluttered with inventions and gadgets. There are cars crowding the highways and too many airplanes in the sky. There are electronic toys in almost every household. Everywhere you look there is someone on a cell phone or checking a pager. We need to ban some of these inventions to make our lives less complicated.

1. **What gadget or invention would you ban? (You may select one mentioned above, or you may think of a different one.)**

   ____

2. **Why would you ban this invention?** _______________________________

   ____

3. **Give two reasons the world would be improved if this invention was banned.**

   a. ____

   b. ____

4. **Write at least one example or detail to support each reason.**

   a. ____

   b. ____

5. **Write a short paragraph persuading world leaders to ban the invention you selected.**

   ____

   ____

   ____

   ____

   ____

  0-7424-1839-1 *Writing to Persuade*

PLANNING A PERSUASIVE PARAGRAPH

Your town's Chamber of Commerce is sponsoring a summer student exchange program. One lucky student in your class will be sent to live with a family in England for the entire summer. They will make their decision based on essays they receive from interested students. You hope they choose you.

To begin putting your essay together, think of some qualities you possess that would make you an ideal candidate (for example, you are adventurous, you like to travel, you adjust easily, you are polite, etc.). List your qualities below. Then think of a specific example from your life that shows this quality.

Quality:____

Example:____

____

Quality: ____

Example: ____

____

Quality: ____

Example: ____

____

Why would you like to be in the student exchange program? Think of three good reasons. Support your reasons with details and examples where possible.

a. ____

b. ____

c. ____

Name _______________________ Date _________

WRITING A PERSUASIVE PARAGRAPH

Write your essay to the Chamber of Commerce persuading them to send you to England this summer. In your paragraph, be sure to include your special qualities and explain why you want to be a summer exchange student. Begin your paragraph with a few facts about yourself. Use your notes from page 54.

0-7424-1839-1 *Writing to Persuade*

Name________________________ Date________________________

UNDERSTANDING BOTH SIDES

If you can understand the reasons behind people's opinions, it may be easier to change their minds. Read the opinions below. For each opinion, write two reasons that support it and two reasons that are against it.

Opinion 1: **Dogs should be confined to a small area when they are home alone.**

Reasons for:
1. ____
2. ____

Reasons against :
1. ____
2. ____

Opinion 2: **There should not be billboards or advertisements along the highway.**

Reasons for:
1. ____
2. ____

Reasons against :
1. ____
2. ____

Opinion 3: **Americans should go to school six days a week.**

Reasons for:
1. ____
2. ____

Reasons against :
1. ____
2. ____

56

0-7424-1839-1 *Writing to Persuade*

Name_________________________ Date____________

SUPPORTING AN OPINION
WITH REASONS AND EXAMPLES

Use the organizer below to write about one of the opinions from page 56 that you feel strongly about. After filling in the organizer, write a persuasive paragraph that explains your opinion. Use specific examples and facts to support your opinion. Use a separate sheet of paper.

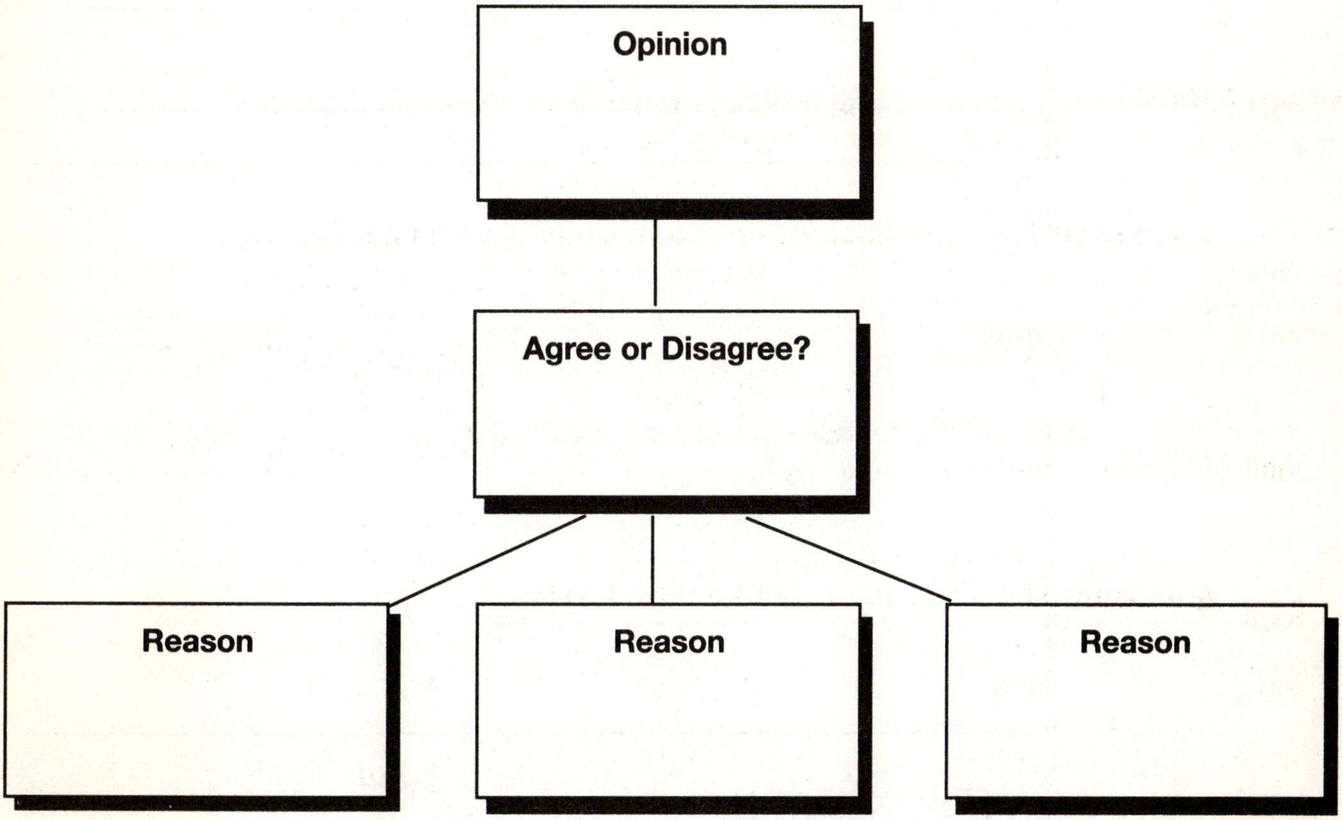

Opinion

Agree or Disagree?

Reason

Reason

Reason

CONSIDERING BOTH SIDES

The students at West Middle School would like to have a volleyball court installed on the playground. They know the principal will be hard to persuade, but they want to present their idea to the principal tomorrow. Before writing the proposal, make some notes below.

Begin by stating reasons the principal will have for not installing the volleyball court. We cannot have a volleyball court because...

1.____

2.____

Now state the reasons why your playground should have a volleyball court. Our playground needs a volleyball court because...

1.____

2.____

3.____

List one or two ways in which the students can be involved in getting a volleyball court. We can help obtain a volleyball court by...

1.____

2.____

On a separate sheet of paper, write your persuasive paragraph for wanting a volleyball court. Include the information from above.

Name_________________________ Date___________

PLANNING AN ARGUMENT

It is report-card time again. You decide to write a paragraph urging the school to do away with report cards. Before writing, think through your argument carefully by filling in the blanks below. Write in complete sentences.

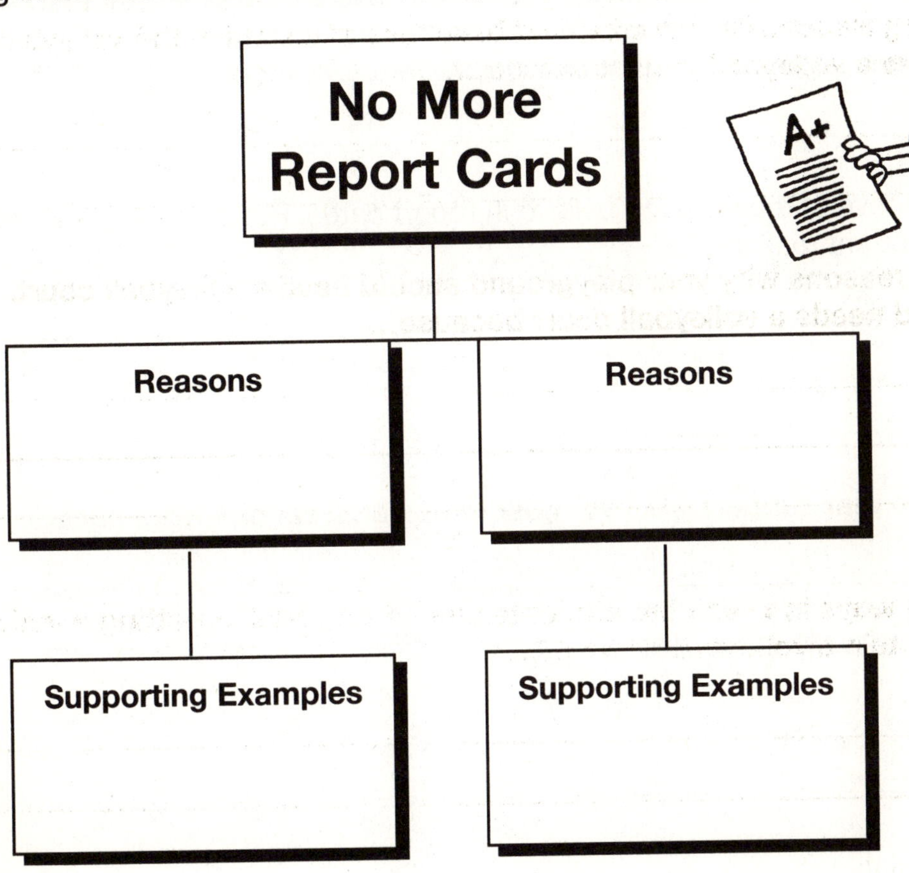

Since schools need some way of grading students, you must suggest a couple alternatives to report cards. List your ideas below.

1. ____

2. ____

Using the information from above, write a few paragraphs persuading your school to stop using report cards. Use a separate sheet of paper. Be sure to suggest a new way of grading students.

CONSIDERING ANOTHER'S POINT OF VIEW

Sometimes it is easier to persuade people if you understand the reasons behind their opinions. Imagine that you work for your school system. You think that report cards are necessary. You want to write a letter to the students explaining why report cards are needed. Organize your thoughts below before writing.

List several reasons you believe in report cards. Put a check mark next to the two most important reasons.

____
____
____

Write examples that support the two most important reasons from above.

Reason #1:_________________________________

Example: ___________________________________

Reason #2: _________________________________

Example: ___________________________________

Write a paragraph that explains two good reasons for using report cards. Support your reasons with examples.

____
____
____
____
____
____
____
____
____

Name_________________________ Date___________

CHOOSING A CAREER

If you could choose your career tomorrow, what would it be? Think about what your interests are. What do you see yourself doing? Do you want to travel? Do you see yourself at a desk? Does helping people or animals interest you?

Fill in the chart below about the career you would choose.

My Career Choice

Why I Chose This Career

Supporting Reason **Supporting Reason** **Supporting Reason**

  0-7424-1839-1 *Writing to Persuade*

WRITING YOUR SPEECH FOR CAREER DAY

You followed your dream, and 20 years later you have the career you wanted when you were younger. Now your 10-year-old son wants you to be a guest speaker on Career Day at his school. Use your notes from page 61 to write your speech. Be persuasive, and try to convince students that this is the career they want. Use examples to excite and interest students.

____

____

____

____

____

____

____

____

____

____

____

____

____

____

____

____

____

____

____

ANSWER KEY

Developing Sentence Images

pages 4–12

Answers will vary.

Writing Advertisements

Identifying Appeal

page 13

1. emotions
2. emotions
3. mind or emotions
4. mind
5. mind
6. emotions
7. mind
8. mind
9. emotions
10. mind

Finding Persuasive Words in Ads

page 14

Wavy Waffles

Wacky, wild Wavy Waffles will <u>bring a smile to your face</u> at the breakfast table. The wavy shapes are <u>fun to eat,</u> and they <u>taste great</u>, too. <u>Drizzle syrup or fruit into the waves and watch it slowly cover your waffle,</u> one wave at a time. Wavy Waffles <u>make breakfast an event</u>. Plain, or covered with butter, syrup, or fruit, Wavy Waffles are <u>sure to be a hit with the whole family.</u>

Ad #1: It appeals to the emotions.

Wavy Waffles

The <u>whole wheat and oats</u> that Wavy Waffles are made of make them a hit with kids and a <u>smart choice for adults. Made of all natural ingredients,</u> they <u>contain little fat</u> and <u>help lower cholesterol</u>. As a part of your diet, Wavy Waffles <u>can help you live a healthier, longer life</u> that has a lot of taste. Try Wavy Waffles and taste what you've been missing. If you're not satisfied, simply return the UPC code to the address on the box and <u>we'll completely refund your money</u>.

Ad #2: It appeals to the mind.

pages 15–22

Answers will vary.

More Analyzing Audiences

page 23

	Teenagers	Adults, 30–40 years old
Spend $ on:	Clothes, food, music, movies	Cars, homes, insurance, travel, furniture, college tuition
Why Save $?:	for college, Christmas gifts, to develop good financial habits	for college tuition, pay bills
Whose opinion matters?:	peers, stars, parents	investment bankers, peers, financial shows
Appealing argument:	Start saving now. You'll have good financial habits, and you'll have money for the future.	If you don't start saving money now, you won't have any money to retire with.
Appealing pictures:	shiny cars, clothes, kids having fun doing things that cost money	adults on vacation, beautiful homes

pages 24–25

Answers will vary.

Persuading with Reasons

Identifying Reasons

page 26

The underlined reasons should be:
1. It has many historic buildings.
2. Many serious accidents occur to small children alone at home.
3. This new book by Debbie Dillinger carefully traces the role of women during the colorful frontier days.
4. Aunt Jenny's muffins are crisp on top and soft and tasty inside.
5. Not enough time is spent on handwriting lessons in elementary schools.
6. Most children in our school do not eat cooked vegetables.
7. Teddy is soft and cuddly. He is the perfect pal for any child.
8. There are amusement rides, farm exhibits, and food-tasting contests.

pages 27–36

Answers will vary.

ANSWER KEY

Writing Letters
Answers will vary.   **pages 37–47**

Supporting Reasons
Identifying Reasons and Supporting Examples   **page 48**

1. People should not litter. It costs taxpayers thousands of dollars each week to clean up the litter. Our town spends $2,000 a week to keep our streets clean.

2. Japanese children go to school six days a week. American school children should also go to school six days a week. This would give students more time to master all the lessons they must learn.

3. Because our school population is growing, our school needs more lockers. This year sixteen students have to share lockers.

4. Everybody should have a garden. Fresh-grown food tastes better. My family will eat beets only if they are picked fresh from the garden.

5. Everyone should collect stamps. It is quite a profitable hobby. A stamp my uncle bought ten years ago for twenty cents just sold for thirty dollars.

More Reasons and Supporting Examples   **page 49**
Author's opinion: School is a good place for children to be.
Reasons:
1. Learn new facts and ideas.
2. People care about you.
3. Friends are there.

Examples:
1. –learned that Columbus was not the first to discover America
2. –classmates made get-well card
   –teacher helped with missed work during lunch
3. –play and talk each day with friends at recess

Answers will vary.   **pages 50–55**

Understanding Both Sides   **page 56**
Opinion 1:
Reasons for:
1. They can't get into as much trouble
2. Helps house-train them
Reasons against:
1. Can't move around very much
2. It is cruel to the animal

Opinion 2:
Reasons for:
1. They are distracting to drivers
2. Some are inappropriate for kids to see
Reasons against:
1. Free speech
2. Gives the public information about stores, politics, issues, and more

Opinion 3:
Reasons for:
1. Get a more thorough education
2. Helps keep us on par with foreign countries
Reasons against:
1. Kids need time off (teachers, too)
2. Adds cost to schools

Answers will vary.   **pages 57–62**

          0-7424-1839-1 *Writing to Persuade*